Brave Enough to Fly to the Moon

SRA

Columbus, OH

SRAonline.com

 SRA

Send all inquiries to this address:
SRA/McGraw-Hill
4400 Easton Commons
Columbus, OH 43219-6188

ISBN: 978-0-07-611696-6
MHID: 0-07-611696-4

1 2 3 4 5 6 7 8 9 RRS 13 12 11 10 09 08 07

The McGraw·Hill Companies

The moon is mysterious. It is out in space. A few brave people have been to the moon!

Traveling to the moon is not easy. How much force will move a spacecraft into space? Scientists needed to find out.

A force is a push or a pull. The force from your feet moves bike pedals. If you pedal fast, it will not take much time to go a long way.

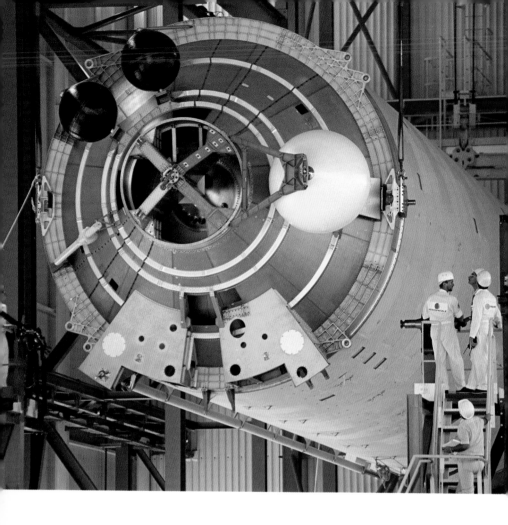

Spacecrafts need enough force to go into space. Scientists learned how much force they need. They learned what way the force should go.

A few brave scientists traveled into space.
Then the United States sent people to the moon!
Three men qualified for the trip.

Neil Armstrong, Buzz Aldrin, and Michael
Collins were ready. The spacecraft was trembling.
It was rumbling too. Then it blasted off!

Soon the spacecraft was in space! Part of the spacecraft landed on the moon. The other part stayed in space.

Armstrong stepped off of the spacecraft. Then Aldrin came leaping out. Their courage helped us learn about the moon.

Vocabulary

mysterious (mis tēr' ē əs) (page 3) *adj.* Difficult to understand or explain.

brave (brāv) (page 3) *adj.* Not afraid.

qualified (kwol' ə fīd') (page 7) *v.* Past tense of **qualify:** To be able to do a job or task.

trembling (trem' bling) (page 8) A form of the verb **tremble:** To shake.

rumbling (rum' bling) (page 8) A form of the verb **rumble:** To make a heavy, deep, rolling sound.

leaping (lēp ing) (page 10) A form of the verb **leap:** To jump.

courage (kûr' ij) (page 10) *n.* The strength to overcome fear.

Comprehension Focus: Asking Questions

1. What do you want to know about riding in a spacecraft to the moon?

2. What would you like to ask the astronauts who walked on the moon?

Activity: Force and Motion

Do this activity to see how the amount of force changes the way an object moves.

What to Do

What You Need
- Masking tape
- Kickball or beach ball

1. Put a piece of tape on the ground. It is your finish line. Sit on the ground a few feet away from the tape.
2. Put the ball on the ground in front of you. Tap the ball. See how far it goes.
3. Use more force. See how much force you need to get the ball to stop on the piece of tape.

What Happened

- How far did the ball go when you tapped it?
- Did you need a large force to get the ball on the tape or a little force?

What If

What if you used a heavy book instead of a ball? Do you think you would need to use more force or less force? Why?